street dance

Liz Gogerly

BL
D1387211

The website addresses (URLs) included in this book were valid at the time of going to press. However, because of the nature of the internet, it is possible that some addresses may have changed, or sites may have changed or closed down since publication. While the author and Publisher regret any inconvenience this may cause the readers, no responsibility for any such changes can be accepted by either the author or the Publisher.

Published in 2013 by Wayland

Copyright © Wayland 2013

Wayland
Hachette Children's Books
338 Euston Road
London NW1 3BH

Wayland Australia
Level 17/207 Kent Street
Sydney NSW 2000

All rights reserved

Concept by Joyce Bentley

Commissioned by Debbie Foy
and Rasha Elsaeed

Produced for Wayland by Calcium
Designer: Paul Myerscough
Editor: Sarah Eason

Photographer: Adam Lawrence

British Library Cataloguing in Publication Data

Gogerly, Liz.
  Street dance: the people, the music,
the moves.
  1. Hip-hop dance—Juvenile literature.
2. Break dancing—
  Juvenile literature.
  I. Title
  793.3-dc22

ISBN: 978 0 7502 7786 0

Every effort has been made to clear copyright.
Should there be any inadvertent omission,
please apply to the publisher for rectification.

Printed in China

Wayland is a division of Hachette Children's
Books, an Hachette UK company.

www.hachette.co.uk

Acknowledgements: Getty Images: Araya
Diaz/WireImage 8, Kerstin Rodgers/Redferns
2c, 11l; Rex Features: W.Disney/Everett 20, ITV
16-17; Shutterstock: Benis Arapovic 3br, 12b,
yakovlev.com 13, Excellent Backgrounds Here
27-27, Andreas Gradin 2–3, 6–7, Kamenetskiy
Konstantin 1, 19t, Olly 18b, 21, Zerra 10.

cover stories

thepeople

themoves

thetalk

MY DREAM JOB

My story by Lois Morris

It all started when I was five. My mum sent me to a dance school where I learned tap, ballet and jazz, as well as singing and acting. At a summer school I went to in my teens, a choreographer spotted me and asked me to audition for a contemporary dance company called *Reflex*. I was a really nervous 14 year old, but I went along to the audition, danced my heart out – and I got in! Over the next two years I travelled the country with the dance company, performing in contemporary dance shows.

In 2009, I decided to try something new and went to the open classes at a local dance academy. They were auditioning dancers for a show, and I guess I must have impressed them because they chose me for a solo performance! On the night of the show I saw the academy's street dance crew perform. They were amazing; really inspirational. I made a pact with myself there and then that by the following year I was going to be one of them. Soon after this, I showed the street dance teacher my stuff – and joined her crew.

The next thing I did was a two-year college course in dance to become a qualified teacher, then I started to teach at the studio where my street dance career began. I've always been totally passionate about a career in dance. It's my dream job and it's what I've always wanted.

Street dance has taught me a lot about what I want from a career, and it's made me determined to be a performer. I'd love to be a backing dancer appearing in music videos or on stage with recording artists. Ultimately, though, I want to be a choreographer and set up my own dance academy. That's my ultimate dream – and I know one day I'll get there...

THE BUZZ ON THE STREETS!

Street dance is funky, energetic and awesome to watch! It's a mish-mash of many dance styles, from hip-hop to jazz to house. There are no rules so street dancers add their own magic steps, known as improvisation. Over the years dance crews have experimented with funk styles, and during the 1970s and 80s added popping and locking moves to their routines. Some added gymnastics, too. Watch out for some crazy backflips and amazing head-spins!

Dance from the streets

Street dance gets its name from the New York streets where it began in the 1970s. Latin and African American gangs held dance competitions or 'dance-offs'. Dancers battled to outdo each other with more and more impressive moves, but they didn't learn these moves in a dance studio. Instead they practised in the street, in the parks, in the clubs and in their bedrooms.

The hip-hop hit!

The rap and hip-hop music scene paved the way for some of the best current street dance styles, including B-boying (or breakdancing), house dance, clowning and krumping. B-boy moves include acrobatic head-spins and fast footwork. Clowning and krumping are more recent dance styles that feature sharp, thrashing or 'clown-like' movements. When it started, street dance was an underground trend, but today it is big news and big business. Street is where it's at!

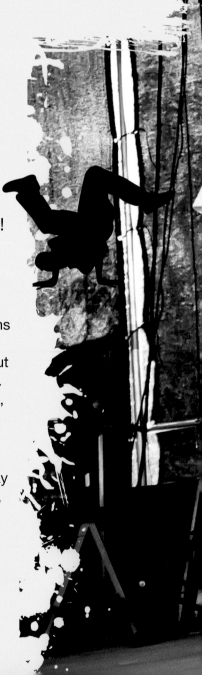

Street dance checklist

- Overall fitness and plenty of energy
- Agility – some moves are pretty tricky
- Self discipline – street dancing needs practice!
- Imagination and new ideas
- Comfortable trainers and some cool, loose gear!

Type 'street dancing' into www.youtube.com to find out what the buzz is all about!

JABBAWOCKEEZ
Street dance crew

THE STATS
Name: JabbaWockeeZ
Group formed: 2003
Hometown: San Diego, California, USA
Job: Street dancers

Starting out

In the beginning, Phil 'Swaggerboy' Tayag, Kevin 'KB' Brewer and Joe 'Emajoenation' Larot formed a trio called *Three Musky*. In 2003, they changed their name to *JabbaWockeeZ* (a.k.a. the *Jabbas*). By 2004, the group was seven-strong and ready to body pop their way to the top.

The *Jabbas* wear identical masks and gloves. This helps the audience to see them as a group instead of individuals.

To watch the *JabbaWockeeZ* in action, search for their videos online.

Go, *Jabbas*, go!

In 2007, the group got their first break on the TV show *America's Got Talent*. They were knocked out early. Later that year, the crew had a terrible shock. Gary Kendall, one of the crew members, died from pneumonia. This made the guys more determined than ever to succeed – they were going to make it for Gary. In 2008, they auditioned for the TV show *America's Best Dance Crew*. Week after week their electrifying hip-hop moves earned them standing ovations. It was no surprise when *JabbaWockeeZ* won best dance crew and bagged $100,000 (over £60,000) prize money.

In a spin

These days, *JabbaWockeeZ* are in great demand. They have starred in Pepsi commercials and in 2008 had a cameo role in the cult street dance movie *Step Up 2: The Streets*. In 2009, they toured with 1980s' pop band *New Kids on the Block*, and a year later the crew wowed the crowds with their own Las Vegas show!

What a crew's gotta do

One of the secrets of the *Jabbas'* success is teamwork and communication. Their tightly synchronised routines are down to hours of practice. The crew make flips and head-spins look easy, but their energetic moves require lots of stamina and determination to keep going. It's that kind of staying power that keeps this dance crew on top.

Career highlights

2008 launched a clothing line, JBWKZ

2009 danced with Shaquille O'Neal in his NBA All-Star Game player intro

2011 founded own record company JBWKZ

2012 track 'FNG' featured on movie soundtrack 'Project X'

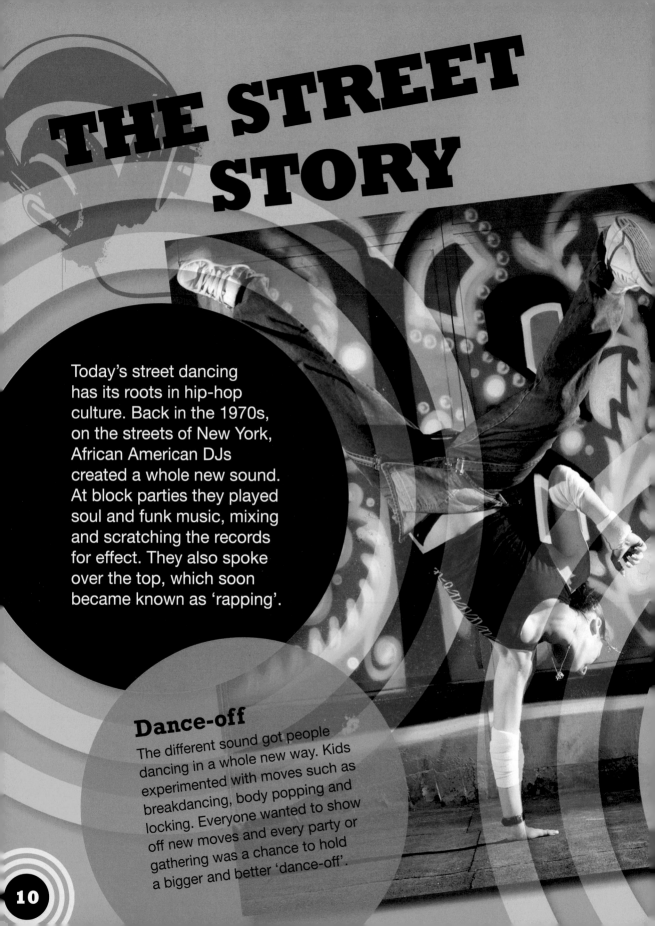

THE STREET STORY

Today's street dancing has its roots in hip-hop culture. Back in the 1970s, on the streets of New York, African American DJs created a whole new sound. At block parties they played soul and funk music, mixing and scratching the records for effect. They also spoke over the top, which soon became known as 'rapping'.

Dance-off

The different sound got people dancing in a whole new way. Kids experimented with moves such as breakdancing, body popping and locking. Everyone wanted to show off new moves and every party or gathering was a chance to hold a bigger and better 'dance-off'.

Breakin' out

Fast forward to the 1980s, and hip-hop music had evolved. The beats were more complicated and rap was where it was at! Street dance moved with the times, too. Michael Jackson's famous 'moonwalk' move and the 1983 blockbuster *Flashdance*, gave hip-hop dance styles mainstream exposure. The new decade introduced many more exciting music styles. People danced to rave, house and techno music. By now street dance had gone global, and all over the world people were enjoying the craze and inventing new steps of their own.

Early street dancers pulled in crowds with their revolutionary dance moves.

Working it out

Gang conflict was ruining lives in some American cities during the 1970s. Dance-offs provided a way for gang members to work through their differences without fighting. At a dance-off two rival gangs called crews would form a circle around two dancers – one from each crew. The two crew members 'danced-off' inside the circle. If the whole crew danced, they formed what is known as an 'apache line' and faced one another as each crew took it in turns to dance. The aim was simple – bust out better, harder and more exciting moves than the rival crew.

From the streets to TV

In the early 1990s, competitive street dance moved away from street gang battles to highly organised events, such as Battle of the Year and Street Dance Weekend. In 1992 Music Television (MTV) created a show called *The Grind*, in which hip-hop culture, music and dance featured. Street dance became prime time TV viewing, and kids everywhere tuned in to watch the hottest dancers work their moves. By the 2000s, street dance was established as the hot new dance to watch. Today, it is a recognised dance form and is taught in dance schools worldwide.

WORDS ON THE STREET

Learn street dance lingo with our fast-track guide!

bashment
a slower-paced street dance often performed to reggae-style music

B-boy
a male dancer who performs breakdancing moves

B-girl
a female dancer who performs breakdancing moves

biting
when someone steals or copies another dancer's moves

burn
to beat someone in a dance-off or 'out-dance' them with a move

clowning
hip-hop moves similar to krumping, but more comical and clown-like

crew
a group of street dancers

'get krunk'
to dance and have a good time

jam
when dancers form a circle and show off their moves at a club or party

krumping
a 'thrashing' style of dance using fast-paced, aggressive movements

locking
a move in which dancers 'lock' or freeze themselves in a certain position

popping
a move in which dancers contract and relax their muscles to create a jerking movement, or 'pop'

top rock
the dance a B-boy or B-girl does while standing, before they go into a floor move

tutting
an angular dance pose. The name comes from 'King Tut' (a slang name for Egyptian Pharaoh Tutankhamun)

xerox
someone who has no original moves and who just copies dance moves created by other dancers

GLOSSARY

agility
the ability to move easily

a.k.a.
this is short for 'also known as'

barracks
a place where soldiers live

block parties
a large public party in a certain neighbourhood or 'block'

breakdance
a dance style normally performed to hip-hop music, with lots of acrobatic moves and ground work

cameo role
a small role as oneself in a performance

choreographer
a dance teacher who creates dance moves and routines

contemporary
around today or a modern form of dancing

evolved
to adapt and change over time

hip-hop
a style of music and dance that originated in the 1970s in the USA

house
a club dance music trend that developed during the 1980s

improvisation
a performance given without planning or preparation

jazz dance
a style of dance that grew out of African American culture in the early 1920s

masterclass
a dance class for experienced or professional dancers

open class
a dance class for dancers of mixed ability

prima ballerina
the leading female ballet dancer in a dance group

rap
a style of music where rhyming lyrics are chanted or spoken along to strong rhythmic backing tracks or music

rave
an electro-synthesised dance music that became popular in the 1980s

scratching
moving vinyl or CDs back and forth on a turntable to create different sounds

stamina
the ability to keep doing something for a long time

synchronise
to coordinate body movements, often in time to music

tap
a dance performed by tapping shoes with steel toes and heels on the ground

techno
an electronic dance music created with software

torso
a person's chest, back and abdomen

underground
hidden or secret; not well known to many people

TOFFEE FROM TRU STREETDANCE

Dancer, choreographer and teacher Ikeela Sealey (a.k.a. Toffee) runs her own street dance academy and organises street dance events. Radar asks Toffee for the urban dance low-down...

Why did you get into street dance?

I first saw a street dance class taking place when I was about 12 years old. It was so exciting! I loved the way dancers created whole new characters for themselves with their facial expressions and moves. I began street dancing not long after and loved it so much that I decided to study contemporary street dance at college.

What music do you dance to?

Everything and anything that's got a beat! The beauty of street dance is that you can tailor it to any kind of music.

What's the best way to start street dancing?

Pluck up your courage, track down a local street dance class and just get dancing! Learn the basics and get a feel for it. Later on you may be able to join a masterclass and dance with the professionals.

Have you ever worked with any famous dancers or singers?

Yes, I've trained dancers and choreographed the routines for music videos for Kanye West and Robbie Williams.

Have you ever won any awards?

In 2007 I won an award for the Youth Dance Choreographer of the Year – the competition was really fierce, so it was great to win.

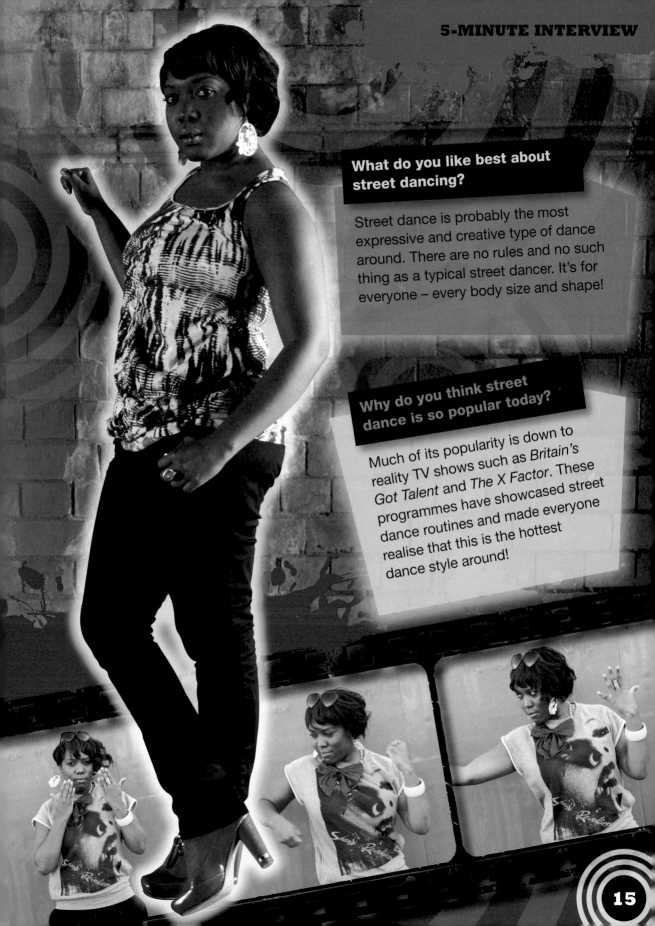

What do you like best about street dancing?

Street dance is probably the most expressive and creative type of dance around. There are no rules and no such thing as a typical street dancer. It's for everyone – every body size and shape!

Why do you think street dance is so popular today?

Much of its popularity is down to reality TV shows such as *Britain's Got Talent* and *The X Factor*. These programmes have showcased street dance routines and made everyone realise that this is the hottest dance style around!

CHERYL COLE

16

THE STATS

Name: Cheryl Cole
Born: 30 June 1983
Place of birth: Newcastle, England, UK
Nationality: British
Job: Pop star

Type 'Cheryl Cole street dance' into www.youtube.com to see some of Cheryl's moves.

Growing up

Cheryl grew up on a council housing estate in Newcastle, UK. She loved singing and dancing, and attended ballet classes from being a young girl. At the age of nine, she was awarded a scholarship to study at a Royal Ballet summer school in London. Cheryl's ambition was to be a prima ballerina!

Flipped out on street dance

Following this, Cheryl took part in another reality TV show: *The Passions of Girls Aloud* in 2008. Each band member was filmed trying out something they had always dreamed of doing. Cheryl's passion was street dance, and the cameras rolled as she underwent training in London and Los Angeles. Her stunning street moves won her a role in hip-hop star will.i.am's *Heartbreaker* music video.

Fight For This Love

A year later, will.i.am produced Cheryl's debut album *3 Words* (2009). The first single from the album, *Fight For This Love*, was used on the soundtrack for the 2010 box office hit *StreetDance 3D*. The single was a smash hit, but it was Cheryl's electrifying street dance routine that sent her solo career sky-high. Following this, she released two more albums, *Messy Little Raindrops* and *A Million Lights*, appeared on the UK and US show *The X Factor*, and reunited with her girl group, *Girls Aloud*.

Girls Aloud and proud

In 2002, Cheryl auditioned for the British reality TV show *Popstars: The Rivals*, and successfully earned herself a place in the winning girl group, *Girls Aloud*. A week later the band stormed to the top of the UK charts with their single *Sound of the Underground*. Cheryl and the band went on to release 13 records that have reached the Top 10 in the UK charts, becoming the most successful reality TV band ever!

STREET MOVES

jacking

downrock

From house dance to hip-hop and B-boying, street dancing is fast, fierce and unforgettable. Here are some of the best of the coolest moves on the street.

Jacking

This is a core house dance move. The dancer bends the knees, or 'jacks', to get the body in position for dance. The upper body can also jack – the dancer moves the torso forwards and backwards, to create a ripple or wave effect.

Downrock

This is a B-boying move in which the dancer places the head, shoulders, elbow or arm on the floor to support the rest of the body above them in a dynamic pose.

Old school freeze

A freeze is a move that a B-boy or B-girl performs to mark the end of a sequence. The dancer can hold it for several seconds before ending the dance or going on to do another set of moves. The old school freeze is a classic B-boy pose in which the dancer places the head, arms and legs on the ground to support the body.

Baby freeze

The dancer uses the arms for support and lifts the legs as high as they can. The move requires upper body strength and must be held for several seconds for maximum impact!

baby freeze

Type 'breakdance freezes' into www.youtube.com and look out for the dancers' amazing freezes.

old school freeze

Briana Evigan and Robert Hoffman step up the heat in the hit dance movie, *Step Up 2: The Streets.*

Search for these amazing music videos online and watch some great street dancing.
• Run DMC vs Jason Nevins: *It's Like That*
• Dizzee Rascal: *Flex*
• Usher: *OMG*
• Mint Royale: *Singing in the Rain*

DANCE CRAZY

Street dancing has exploded onto the scene through TV, movies, advertising and the internet. Those hot steps, cool body pops and way-out flips add up to big business! Read on...

Movie magic

The UK *StreetDance 3D* and the US *Step Up 3D* were smash hits in 2010. Mixing up hip-hop and other dance moves, they took street dance to a whole new level and a new generation of fans was created. But street dance does not have to be three-dimensional to leap out of the screen. Look out for *B-Girl* (2008), *Boogie Town* (2009), the original *Step Up* movie from 2006 and the dramatic follow-up, *Step Up 2: The Streets (2008).*

The hip-hop artist Chris Brown describes street dance as '... more than just a way of moving, it's a different expression of music.'

TV Dreams

In 2008, 14-year-old *Britain's Got Talent* champion George Sampson captured the nation's interest with his street dance routine. The following year, dance crews *Diversity* and *Flawless* battled it out in the semi-finals. Kids everywhere were inspired to give street dancing a go. The first ever *America's Best Dance Crew* hit our TV screens in 2008. The winning crew *JabbaWockeeZ*, began to sell out concert venues worldwide.

Many other street dance crews have wowed audiences since, including *Jungle Boogie*, a six-member crew led by pint-sized female dancer Raqi, and the winners of 2010 *America's Best Dance Crew*, the all-Asian dance group *Poreotix*.

Popping pop stars

Many of the world's biggest pop stars have also got in on the street dance act. Everyone from Justin Timberlake and Beyoncé to Chris Brown and the Chemical Brothers feature street dance scenes in their music videos. Many top recording dance artists feature street dance in their tours, music videos and promotional material. When it comes to fusing creativity with selling power, the music industry is following the street beat.

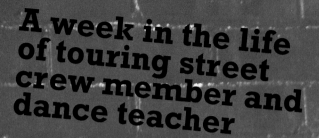

A week in the life of touring street crew member and dance teacher

ELIJAH HUNTER

Sunday

Today was a great day, but totally exhausting! I had a five-hour training session with my dance crew, working on a routine that we've been practising for a couple of weeks. It is almost perfect, so we were really happy with it, even if we were pretty done in!

Monday

I spent today at the studio, working on my bashment, popping and breakdance. Tonight we had a jam session. We made a circle, put on some music and took it in turns to dance in the middle. It's a great excuse to show off some moves. The energy was sparking off all the other dancers and the whole atmosphere was really electric!

Tuesday

This morning was all about prepping our routines for our performance this evening at Sandhurst Military

blog   news   events

Academy in Surrey, UK. We wanted it to be step-perfect, so every second of rehearsals counted. It paid off. We put on a really dynamic show in the evening and the crowd down at the barracks seemed really impressed!

Wednesday

Today I just chilled out at home. I really needed it after last night's full-on performance. I headed back to the studio in the evening to teach my contemporary and street classes. I love teaching these sessions, so I really pushed myself tonight, even though my muscles were still aching from last night's show!

Thursday

What a great day! We had an open class session and it was my turn to teach. The pace was really fast and the dancers had loads of energy. It rubbed off on the whole crew and we put in a really hot dance session afterwards.

Saturday

Back to school today! We were booked to teach at a local school, so I took the first workshop. Then the crew and I did a street dance session for the kids. They really loved it and we've been invited back to do another session next year. It feels like all the effort and hard work is paying off when we get this kind of response!

JACKING AND JERKING

This basic step is used in many street dance routines, so it's a great one to master. It's broken down into stages here, but put it all together and you have the basis for a great move!

You will need:

- space to dance
- comfortable clothing and shoes

1

Start the jack with your feet apart. Lean forwards and bend your knees.

2

Lean your body back a little while still bending your knees. This completes the jack move.

3

Get set for the jerk. Straighten your legs and kick your right leg out in front of your body.

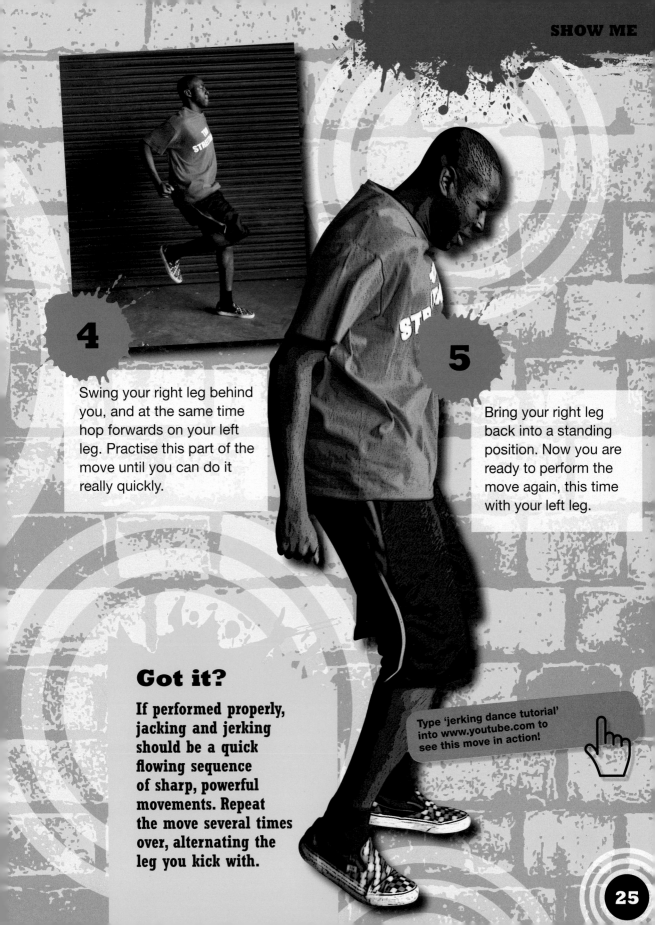

4

Swing your right leg behind you, and at the same time hop forwards on your left leg. Practise this part of the move until you can do it really quickly.

5

Bring your right leg back into a standing position. Now you are ready to perform the move again, this time with your left leg.

Got it?

If performed properly, jacking and jerking should be a quick flowing sequence of sharp, powerful movements. Repeat the move several times over, alternating the leg you kick with.

Type 'jerking dance tutorial' into www.youtube.com to see this move in action!

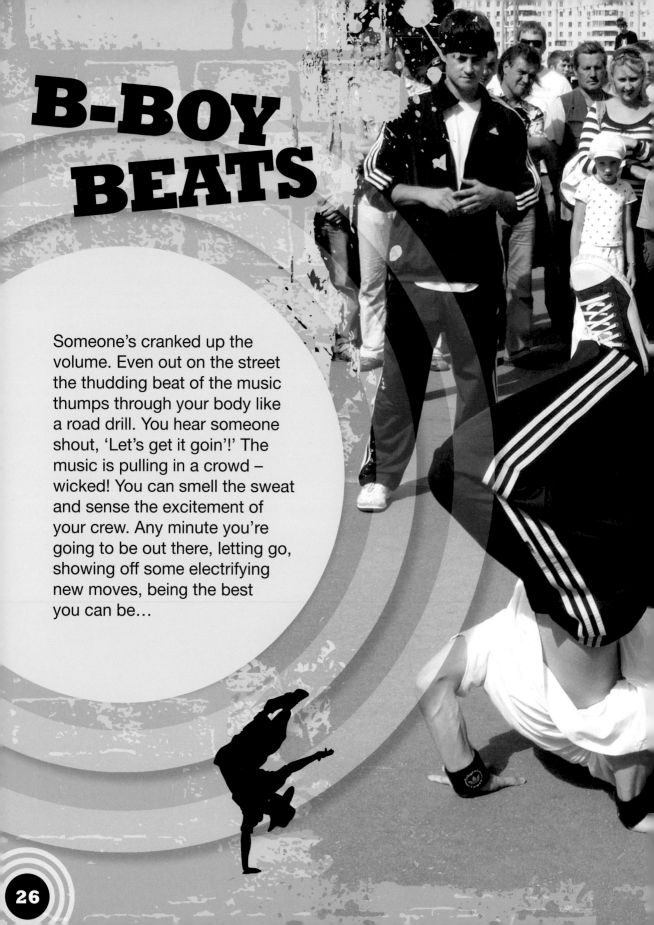

B-BOY BEATS

Someone's cranked up the volume. Even out on the street the thudding beat of the music thumps through your body like a road drill. You hear someone shout, 'Let's get it goin'!' The music is pulling in a crowd – wicked! You can smell the sweat and sense the excitement of your crew. Any minute you're going to be out there, letting go, showing off some electrifying new moves, being the best you can be…

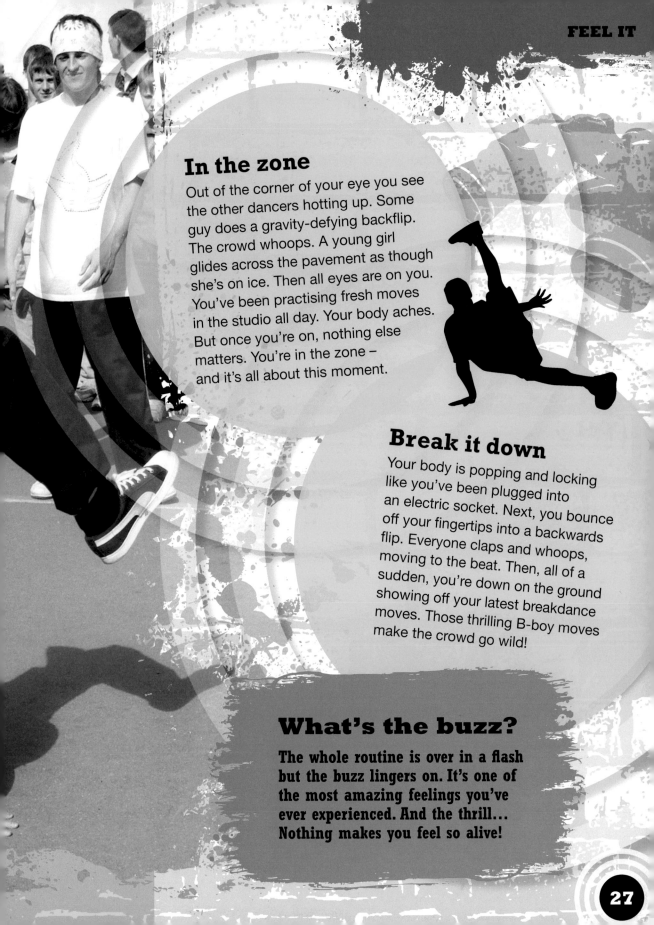

In the zone

Out of the corner of your eye you see the other dancers hotting up. Some guy does a gravity-defying backflip. The crowd whoops. A young girl glides across the pavement as though she's on ice. Then all eyes are on you. You've been practising fresh moves in the studio all day. Your body aches. But once you're on, nothing else matters. You're in the zone – and it's all about this moment.

Break it down

Your body is popping and locking like you've been plugged into an electric socket. Next, you bounce off your fingertips into a backwards flip. Everyone claps and whoops, moving to the beat. Then, all of a sudden, you're down on the ground showing off your latest breakdance moves. Those thrilling B-boy moves make the crowd go wild!

What's the buzz?

The whole routine is over in a flash but the buzz lingers on. It's one of the most amazing feelings you've ever experienced. And the thrill... Nothing makes you feel so alive!

27

BODY LOCKING

Body locking is a combination of quick movements and sharp, angular shapes created by 'locking' your limbs into a 'frozen' pose. You 'lock' by holding your joints in a firm and fixed position.

You will need:

- **space to dance**
- **comfortable clothing and shoes**

1

Roll your hands up to head level (palms face forwards) and 'lock' your elbows and wrists into the position shown above.

2

Push your hands down to hip height, with palms facing down. 'Lock' your arms and wrists into the position shown above.

3

Lean forward, pull your hands up along with your right knee. This should be completed in one move. 'Lock' your arms and legs into the position shown above.

4

Hop on to your right foot and push your right arm out to the side, point your finger and 'lock' into position.

5

Place your left foot on the ground, push out your left arm and point your finger. 'Lock' into position.

Got it?

Steps 1–5 should make a fluid sequence. Your moves should be short and sharp, with your wrists, knees and elbows locked.

Type 'popping and locking' into www.youtube.com to see some amazing moves!

HOUSE STEP

The house music trend of the 1980s inspired this street dance move. So why not crank up the house and give it a go?

You will need:

• **space to dance**
• **comfortable clothing and shoes**

1

Lift your right leg to one side and put your left hand on your right shoulder.

2

Bring your right leg down and cross it behind your left. At the same time, slide your left hand down and across your body.

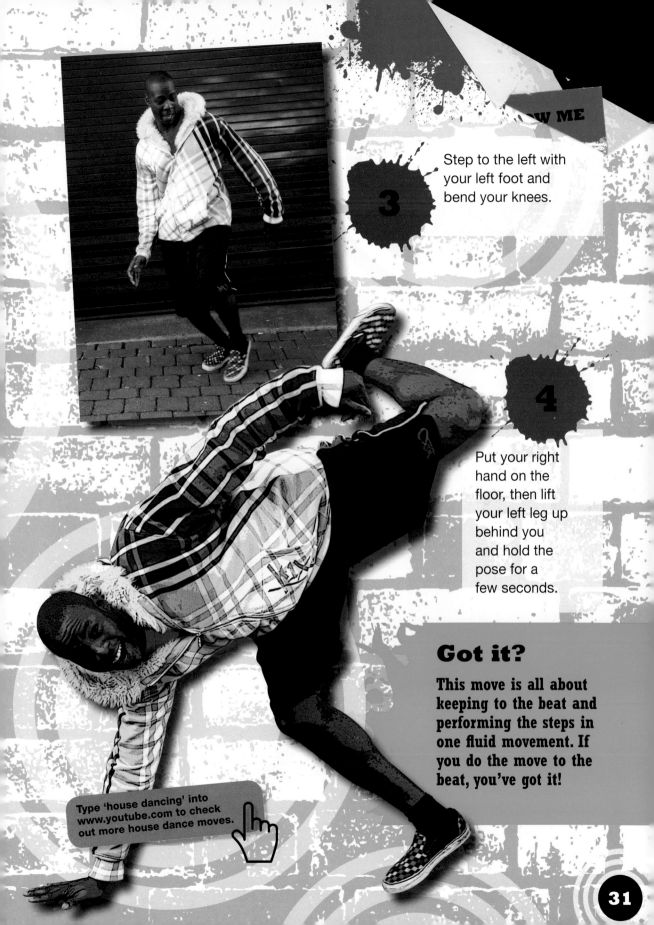

3 Step to the left with your left foot and bend your knees.

4 Put your right hand on the floor, then lift your left leg up behind you and hold the pose for a few seconds.

Got it?

This move is all about keeping to the beat and performing the steps in one fluid movement. If you do the move to the beat, you've got it!

Type 'house dancing' into www.youtube.com to check out more house dance moves.

BUST SOME MOVES!

People to talk to

Get into the hottest dance style around and get fit while having fun! Street dance classes and clubs are opening up all over the country. Search Street Dance UK (www.streetdanceuk.com) for a venue near you. You could be a few steps away from a whole new crew!

Tru Streetdance Academy

Take classes from the master street dance teachers at Tru Streetdance. Find classes, fun events, inspirational dance shows and more at:
www.trustreetdance.com

Dance-offs today

Check out the UDO World Street Dance Championships and the World Street Dance Festival at:
www.udoworlds.webs.com
www.juste-debout.com

Books & Apps

Hip Hop and Street Dance, Jane Bingham (Heinemann, 2008)

Street Dance: Master This, Emma Torrington (Wayland, 2010)

Download the latest iStreetDance apps at:
www.istreetdance.co.uk.

INDEX